LOOSE CHANGE

A GUIDE TO COMMON COINS AND MEDALS

EDWARD BESLY

AMGUEDDFEYDD AC ORIELAU CENEDLAETHOL CYMRU

NATIONAL MUSEUMS & GALLERIES OF WALES

CARDIFF 1997

First Published in 1997
© National Museum of Wales
Cathays Park
Cardiff CF1 3NP

ISBN: 0 7200 0444 6

Design and production: Arwel Hughes
Type: New Baskerville
Printing: Zenith Media

Title page: A hoard comes to light
(J. Y. Akerman *Coins of the Roman Empire relating to Britain* 1844)

INTRODUCTION

In 1973 the National Museum of Wales published a booklet by the late George C. Boon, *A Hundred and One Coins*, an illustrated guide to the coins and tokens most commonly brought to the Museum for identification. This most useful work is long since out of print, but the need remains, so the opportunity has therefore been taken to produce, in effect, a second edition, revised, expanded and updated.

The present work has two aims: firstly to present common coins within a chronological framework; and secondly to place these coins in their historical and currency contexts. The emphasis remains on common types, many of which are frequently brought for identification, but some coins are included which may be quite rare, but are helpful in placing the others in context. Occasionally, a rare specimen may nevertheless serve to illustrate a common class. The choice of what to include is a personal one, a curator's choice, based on experience in Wales since 1986, and while examples of Welsh relevance have been used wherever possible, readers such as museum curators should be able readily to identify the related types from their own areas. My perception of what is common is somewhat different from that of twenty-four years ago, so some specimens have disappeared, while new types have been included. New discoveries and the development of the Museum's coins and medals collection have also made fresh material available to draw upon. A few common medals have also been included.

The arrangement of the text follows in large measure that of the Coins and Medals gallery at the National Museum & Gallery Cardiff, where many of the specimens illustrated here - and much else - may be viewed on display. Unless indicated otherwise, specimens are illustrated life size. Technical 'numismatic' terms are in general avoided, but a short glossary explains those that have been included. Where the provenance (find spot) of a coin is known, this is given in italics.

GLOSSARY OF TERMS

Billon
an alloy of silver containing less than 50% of silver

Clipping
illegal removal of metal from the edge of a coin

Counterfeit
a false coin intended for circulation

Debasement
reduction of the precious-metal content of a coin, by lowering its issue weight or adding base metal such as copper to the alloy

Demonetisation
removal from circulation by withdrawal of 'legal tender' status

Die
an engraved metal block used to impress the design of a coin

Fineness
the proportion of precious metal in an alloy; usually expressed as a percentage, or as parts per thousand

Hammered coinage
coinage produced by hand

Milled coinage
coinage produced by machinery

Moneyer
the official responsible for producing a coin (not always the workman who makes it)

Obverse
the 'heads' side of a coin, or that which bears the name of the ruler or issuer; ~ die: in hammered coinage usually the lower, or anvil die.

Privy-mark
a letter, symbol or other mark added to the dies to identify the mint or (especially) period of issue of a coin, for internal mint control purposes

Recoinage
the replacement of existing coinage by recalling it and reminting, usually with different designs

Reverse
the 'tails' side of a coin; ~ die: in hammered coinage, usually the upper (hand-held) die

BRITISH WEIGHTS

1 Pound Troy = 12 ounces = 373.24 grammes

1 Ounce Troy = 20 pennyweights (dwt);
1 dwt = 24 grains (gr)

1 Pound Avoirdupois = 16 ounces = 453.59 grammes

BRITISH MONETARY SYSTEMS

before 1971
1 Pound (£) = 20 shillings (s) = 240 pence (d)

1 Mark = 13s 4d (160d)

since 1971
1 Pound (£) = 100 pence (p)

THE ANCIENT WORLD

The use of weighed quantities of silver for payments is recorded in the Middle East over 4,000 years ago, but coins - pieces of metal of fixed weights and alloys, marked (and thus guaranteed) by their issuers - were first produced in Lydia (present-day western Turkey) in the seventh century BC. Within a hundred years, the use of coinage was widespread in the Greek world.

The earliest coinages were of small ingots, impressed with a design. They were made by striking the ingots against an engraved anvil using iron punches: these left their own marks, so the idea of using a second engraved 'die' led to the evolution of coins as we would recognise them today - circular discs with designs in relief on both sides.

Ancient coins in silver and gold are not commonly encountered as museum enquiries, except as replicas or fakes, but the extensive copper alloy small change of Greek states, especially of Ptolemaic Egypt, is frequently seen.

1. Lydia, Sardes: silver half-stater, *c*.550 BC.
An early silver coin which retains an ingot-like form, its reverse bearing the impression of two square punches.

2. Athens: silver tetradrachm, 5th century BC.
This 'dollar' of the ancient world was produced in huge numbers from the silver mined at Laurion, in Athenian territory. Because of its general acceptance as a trading coin, it was also widely imitated. The 'heads and tails' idea, here depicting Athens's patron deity and her symbols, persists in many coinages to the present. True likenesses of rulers emerged on the coinages of the Hellenistic kingdoms in the third century BC.

3. Macedonia: bronze coin of Alexander the Great, 336-323 BC.
Token coinages in bronze were adopted in parts of the Greek world from the fifth century BC. Large numbers survive, often in poor or worn condition. There are many thousands of designs. Here, Alexander the Great identifies himself with the hero Herakles (Hercules) and his weapons.

4. Egypt: bronze coin of Ptolemy IV, 221-205 BC.
The dynasty established by Ptolemy I (c.304-283 BC), one of Alexander the Great's generals, lasted until Cleopatra (51-30 BC). The designs of Egyptian bronze coins varied little for over 200 years. All bore the name Ptolemy, and several sizes occur. They did not circulate outside Egypt, but are frequently brought into museums in Britain for identification (see no.**22**).

5. Roman Republic: silver denarius of P. Crepusius, *c.*80 BC.
This characteristic Roman Republican coin was introduced around 211 BC. Repetitive images, such as the head of Roma, the Dioscuri (the heavenly twins Castor and Pollux), or a figure of victory in a chariot, were supplemented, and eventually superseded by a rich variety of designs of personal or family significance, chosen by the three moneyers, who were middle-ranking officials responsible for the coinage, appointed annually. Since Republican denarii circulated until the early second century AD, they are frequently found in Britain, usually in worn condition. Some of them have a 'serrated' edge: this was an attempt to prevent forgery - to show that the coin was not plated base metal - which apparently failed.

The Greek World

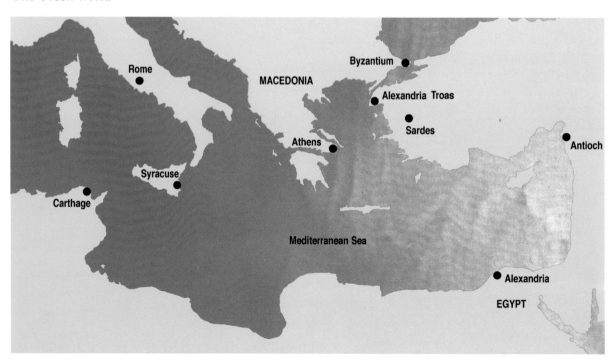

6. Armorica (north-western Gaul): base silver stater of the Coriosolitae, 1st century BC.

The Celtic world probably first encountered coinage in payments for mercenary service in the Mediterranean area. When their paymasters were conquered by the Romans, the Celts produced their own coins, usually copying familiar Greek designs. In Gaul and Britain, most coins imitated gold staters of Philip II of Macedon (359-36 BC), which depicted the head of Apollo and a two-horse chariot. Celtic artists produced numerous variations on this theme, even in base metals, perhaps because of the significance of the (severed?) head and of the horse in their society. Many coins bear no legends to indicate their issuers, so the archaeological record provides valuable clues as to their origins, and there are occasional references to Celtic coinage by contemporary commentators such as Julius Caesar in the 50s BC.

7. Southern Britain: silver 'unit' of Eppillus, 'king' of the Atrebates.
The last flowering of Celtic coinage was in Britain. In the half-century before the Roman conquest began in AD 43, many designs were created which owed much to increasing cultural and commercial contacts with the Roman world. Rulers are named, sometimes even their mints - here, *Calleva* (Silchester, in north Hampshire).

THE ROMAN EMPIRE

At its height in the second century AD the Roman Empire stretched from Britain to the Middle East, taking in much of Europe and North Africa. From the time of Augustus (27 BC - AD 14) a highly-organised currency of gold, silver and copper alloys was used for transactions at all levels (box). In the west, this replaced all previous coinages, but the cities of the east - the Greek world - still issued their own small change for local circulation and the province of Egypt continued a separate monetary system. After two centuries of relative stability, the decline of the Augustan system was hastened by the military and economic pressures of the third century AD, and it finally collapsed around 270.

Roman imperial coins almost invariably bear an emperor's portrait, name and titles; their reverses depict a range of gods, 'virtues', imperial 'victories' or other designs which are sometimes of great historical interest.

The Imperial Monetary System		
1 gold aureus =	*2 gold quinarii =*	*25 silver denarii*
1 denarius =	*2 silver quinarii =*	*4 brass sestertii*
1 sestertius =	*2 brass dupondii =*	*4 copper asses*
1 as =	*2 semisses =*	*4 quadrantes*

8. Silver Denarius of Hadrian, AD 117-38.

Boverton hoard, Vale of Glamorgan

The denarius was the 'penny' or day's pay of the Biblical vineyard labourer [Matthew, ch.20], or just over a day's pay for a second-century legionary soldier, before deductions. On the reverse FELICITAS denotes prosperity or success.

9. Sestertius of Trajan, AD 98-117.

Caerwent, Monmouthshire

This fine example of Roman coin-making is also a superb 'archaeological' coin, found in the construction levels of the *forum-basilica* (market-place) of Roman Caerwent (*Venta Silurum*). The rare historical subject of this coin is Trajan's new harbour at Ostia, the port of Rome, which was completed around AD 112, and is shown here complete with warehouses, ships, statues - and even the bollards and fenders of the quays. The 'sestertius' was also the standard unit of account in the early Empire.

10. Dupondius of Marcus Aurelius, AD 161-80.

Unprovenanced

The legends of this coin give an abbreviated series of the emperor's titles: his 30th tribunician year (which dates the coin to AD 175-6), 8th imperial acclamation and 3rd consulship; the figure of Aequitas (fairness or probity) on the reverse is sometimes identified with the mint itself. The ruler's 'radiate' crown, a sign of divinity, was also used to indicate a 'double' denomination (here, 2 asses). The distinctive headgear worn by the emperors and the different coloured metals (not always obvious today) usually serve to distinguish the similarly-sized dupondii and asses.

11. As of Claudius, AD 41-54.

Rodd Nant, Powys

On the as, the emperor is shown bareheaded or wearing a laurel wreath. The large letters S C refer to a senatus-consultum, or senatorial decree, indicating the Senate's responsibility for the base metal coinage. Inadequate supplies of small change to the army in Britain following the initial invasion of AD 43 led to widespread local copying of these asses, which depict the goddess Minerva. In Wales, pre-Flavian (i.e., before AD 69) coins are generally scarce and are often a good sign of early military activity.

12. 'Radiate', or double-denarius of Philip I , AD 244-9.
   Bassaleg hoard, near Newport

13. Debased radiate of Gallienus, sole reign AD 260-8.
   Llanedeyrn hoard, near Cardiff

The 'radiate', introduced by Caracalla in 215 to help meet an increase in army pay, weighed 1½ denarii, but was probably worth two. By now, the fineness of the 'silver' coinage was around 50% , and this continued to fall, concealed by careful minting practice until the 250s. By the early 260s, with finenesses below 15%, the mints were obliged to apply silver washes to the surfaces of new coins.

14-16. Radiates of the Gallic usurpers: Victorinus, 269-71; Tetricus I and II, 271-4. *Llanedeyrn hoard*

From 260 to 274, Britain belonged to a breakaway Gallic state, established by Postumus, governor of Germany, who until 268 maintained a 'silver' coinage around 15% fine. Thereafter, massive issues of base coins, containing less than 5% silver, dominated British circulation for two decades, driving out of circulation virtually all silver coins as well as the copper-alloy denominations of the Augustan system. The Romano-Gallic empire survived several attempts at reconquest before its last rulers surrendered to Aurelian in 274.

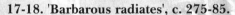

17-18. 'Barbarous radiates', c. 275-85.
   Llanedeyrn hoard

Aurelian (270-5) carried out a partial monetary reform, which mainly improved the appearance of the coinage. Supplies of new coin to Britain and northern Gaul seem to have been totally inadequate and these areas saw an 'epidemic' of illegal copying of the current coinage. These coins are known as barbarous radiates and are easily recognised from their crude style: the worst may be tiny or downright illiterate.

19. 'Radiate' of Carausius, AD 286/7-93, London mint?
Little Orme hoard, North Wales

20. 'Quinarius' of Allectus, AD 293-6, C mint.

Carausius, admiral of the Channel fleet was driven to rebel, it is said, fearing retribution for his practice of capturing pirate ships only after they had raided the coasts he was paid to protect. He held Britain and, at first, parts of northern Gaul. His mints at London, Rouen and elsewhere rapidly produced a crude and distinctive coinage, often overstruck on older coins, initially mostly with no mint signature. Later coins, and those of Allectus - his finance minister who eventually murdered him - are often of fine style. Two main mints signed L (clearly London) and C (or G? - location still unknown). Base metal coins of the 'British Empire' are fairly common, but the rarity of silver (reintroduced briefly by Carausius) and gold of both rulers testifies the efficiency with which these were suppressed following reconquest of the island in 296.

21. Alexandria Troas (Turkey), local bronze coin issued under Roman rule.

The obverse shows the emperor Trebonianus Gallus, AD 251-3. The emperor's name and titles are here in Latin, but on most local coinages in the east are given in Greek. The reverses of these 'Greek Imperials' often depict subjects of more than purely local interest: here the city council is shown in session.

Roman Caerwent: the *curia* or council chamber of the *basilica*, excavated in 1988, showing channels in the floor for the wooden benches of the tribal council of the native Silures.

22. Egypt, tetradrachm of Probus, AD 276-82.

Coinage purely for use in Egypt continued to be made at Alexandria under the Romans. The silver became heavily debased and the later third century coins are very common indeed. On the reverse, the symbols 'L B' represent the regnal year, which at Alexandria began on 29 August: here 'year 2' = 276/7. Typically these are thick coins with rough edges. These coins did not circulate outside Egypt, but many have been brought to Britain by tourists and servicemen since the eighteenth century, and they are often 'dug up' in parks and gardens, having been lost in recent times. Twenty have even been recovered from the wreck of *H.M.S. Pomone*, a frigate wrecked in 1811 on the Needles, Isle of Wight, returning from duties in the eastern Mediterranean.

THE LATER ROMAN EMPIRE

In 293-4, Diocletian reformed the Roman coinage, unifying the whole Empire, replacing the local issues of the east and by 296 bringing Egypt into the system. A network of mints, from London to Alexandria, produced coins of common designs and standards, distinguished mostly by explicit mint signatures. Continuing inflationary pressures led to repeated changes in standards, most obviously observed in progressive weight reductions of the everyday coinage, interrupted by occasional reforms, for instance in 348. There seems to have been a strong revival in the use - or least the hoarding - of fine silver coins in Britain in the later fourth century.

Mints of the later Roman Empire

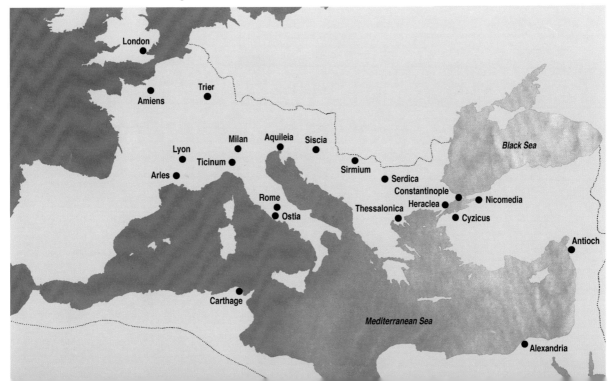

The Tetrarchic (four rulers) system of Diocletian and the family hierarchies of Constantine the Great (306-37) and Valentinian I (364-75) resulted in simultaneous coinages for several rulers, coupled with small numbers of populist reverse designs which were used for several years at a time.

23. **Nummus of Diocletian, AD 284-305, Trier mint.**
24. **Nummus of Maximian, AD 284-305, Alexandria mint.**
25. **Nummus of Constantius I, AD 293-306, unsigned (London mint).**
    Bridgend hoard

The first 'single currency', *nummi* were bronze coins of around 10 grammes, containing about 3-4% of silver and with silver-coated surfaces. At first, almost all bore the message GENIO POPVLI ROMANI ('to the spirit of the Roman people'), although coins minted at Carthage had their own designs of local significance. Apart from a few signed 'LON', coins struck at London bore no mint name until *c*.306, but their style and find spots make the attribution secure.

26-28. Nummi of Constantine I, AD 306-37.

Llanbethery hoard, Vale of Glamorgan

These are some of the commonest Roman coins found in Britain. By 330, when these designs were introduced, a long decline in the nummus had reduced it to a coin of about 2 grammes. 'Constantinopolis' (**26**) and 'Urbs Roma' (**27**) commemorated the two capitals of the Empire, following the elevation of the first, formerly known as Byzantium, as eastern capital in 330: no.**27** depicts Rome's legendary founders, Romulus and Remus. By now, the London mint had closed, so Trier (**26**), Lyon (**27**) and Arles ('Constantia', no.**28**) in Gaul were the main sources of Britain's currency.

29-30. Maiorina of Constantius II, AD 337-61, and a contemporary counterfeit.
Llys Awel, Abergele.

A reform in AD 348, the 1100th anniversary of Rome's foundation, introduced new, larger, small change of several designs, which all proclaimed FEL TEMP REPARATIO (roughly, 'happy times are here again'). Poor supply to Britain during the 350s led to another outbreak of widespread copying, mostly of this 'soldier and fallen horseman' type. Once thought to be sub-Roman (i.e., fifth century), even the smallest of these counterfeits have been shown through secure archaeological contexts to be roughly contemporary with their prototype.

31. Bronze of Valens, AD 364-78.
Llys Awel, Abergele

Coins of the 370s are the latest found regularly in Wales, though at the Roman town at Caerwent hoards and single coins include issues down to the end of the century. The lead-containing bronzes of the latest Roman coins are often badly made and poorly preserved. In common with the rest of Britain, coin use in Wales ceased when the Romans departed in AD 410.

THE BYZANTINE EMPIRE

Despite its eclipse in the West by the fifth century, the Roman Empire survived in the East, with its capital at Constantinople until it finally fell to the Turks in 1453. Byzantine coins were principally struck in gold and copper, and the latter are frequently encountered, having arrived in Britain in more recent times.

32. Follis of Justin I, AD 518-27.

In AD 498, the emperor Anastasius completely reformed the smaller currency, creating the 'typical' Byzantine coinage. Copper coins of 40, 20, 10 and 5 noumia (i.e., nummi) were introduced, with prominent marks of value - M, K, I and E respectively - and clear mint-marks (here 'delta'/ CON, indicating the fourth workshop of the Constantinople mint.

33. 'Anonymous' follis, class A2, attributed to Basil II and Constantine VIII, AD 976-1025.

Between about 970 and 1060 Byzantine copper coins bore no emperors' names or portraits, merely an image of Christ and his titles 'Jesus Christ, King of Kings', or similar. Successive issues were often restruck on the previous, a feature which has helped to determine their sequence and approximate dates.

THE MIDDLE AGES

After the Romans left, Britain remained coinless for two centuries, but from the seventh century AD the emerging Anglo-Saxon kingdoms began to produce and use coinages consisting of silver pennies. Around 973-5, King Edgar's reform created a unified national coinage of a single design, on which the mints and moneyers were always identified. The obverse usually bore a stylised portrait of the king together with his name and titles, while the reverse designs were almost always based on a cross. Only a single design of coin was current at a given time and every few years this was changed, necessitating a complete recoinage at a network of mints across the country (90, not all of which were open at once) - a useful fiscal device for the monarch, who took a tax on each occasion.

The Norman conquerors of 1066 maintained this system, but from late in the reign of Henry I (1100-35), regular recoinages gave way to 'immobilised' designs, the use of which might span more than one reign. Some of these were very long-lived: the 'Short Cross' coinage of 1180-1247; the 'Long Cross' types of 1247-78; and Edward I's 'sterling' coinage of 1279, which introduced designs that remained in use for over two hundred years.

Regional and subsequent central production of the dies gave the coinage an essential uniformity which together with evidence from hoards has proved vital in the fine dating of coins of the later series.

34. Silver penny of Æthelred II, 978-1016, Lydford mint (Devon), moneyer Bruna. *St Lythans, near Cardiff*

This coin was probably current c.1003-1009. The King's portrait is a direct copy of certain late third-century Roman coins, and gives rise to the modern description, the 'Helmet' type. On the reverse, a small cross indicates the beginning of the legend. Few pre-conquest coins are found in Wales, and there were no Welsh mints until the 1080s, when small issues were made at Cardiff, Rhuddlan, St Davids (probably) and Abergavenny (perhaps). A single coin is known in the name of a Welsh ruler - a coin of Hywel Dda ('the Good', died c.950), which was probably an honorific issue struck at Chester in the 940s.

35. 'Short Cross' penny, c.1205-9, Lincoln mint, moneyer Hue. *Llanfaes, Anglesey*

Coins of this type, all bearing the name 'Henry', span the reigns of Henry II (d.1189), Richard I (1189-99), John (1199-1216) and Henry III (1216-72). Detailed study of the coins, singly and in hoards, and of associated documentary evidence has enabled them to be fairly closely dated. By now the mints had been reduced to 22, though, recoinages apart, only London and Canterbury continued to be important. In Wales, there were occasional issues of Short Cross pennies at Rhuddlan, and these started before 1195, when the town was controlled by the native Welsh princes of Gwynedd.

36. 'Long Cross' penny, *c.*248-50, London mint, moneyer Nichole.
Llanfaes, Anglesey

One impetus to the change of design in 1247 may have been widespread clipping of the previous coinage. By extending the cross to the very edge of the reverse and allowing circulation only of those coins where the tips of the cross could be seen it was hoped to deter this, but the practice continued unabated. Many pairs of letters on these coins are ligatured, i.e., joined together; this and the loss of the initial cross often makes them harder to identify in detail.

37-38. Long Cross cut halfpenny, moneyer Willem, and farthing, London mint. *Llanfaes, Anglesey*

Before 1280, very few coins smaller than the penny were produced. For smaller transactions, therefore, coins were often cut into halves and quarters, using the cross on the reverse as a guide. It is often not possible to identify the parent coins precisely. It is hard to compare values in very different economic systems, but with a silver penny equivalent to several pounds today, even a cut farthing represents a significant sum.

Llanfaes, Anglesey.
Now a small village, Llanfaes was during the thirteenth century the commercial centre and port of the native Welsh principality of Gwynedd, boasting fairs and a weekly market, but by 1305 the town had ceased to exist. Edward I removed its inhabitants to Rhosyr, about twelve miles away, and its buildings were dismantled and rebuilt at the new town of Beaumaris nearby. Recent metal-detected finds have produced dramatic evidence for the location and the extent of coin-use and commercial activity at this site. (*E. Besly*)

39. Penny of Edward I, Canterbury mint, 1280s.
Llanfaes, Anglesey

A further recoinage in 1279 saw fundamental changes. New denominations were introduced: round halfpence (see **100**) and farthings, and the groat of fourpence, though this last was not a success. The mint was still identified, but the name of the moneyer no longer appeared. Because three successive kings called Edward issued coins of the same designs (until 1377), close dating of their coins depends upon study of hoards and of the punches used to sink the dies: for instance, fifteen consecutive classes of pennies have been identified for Edward I and II, the first nine of which have crowns with the fleurs-de-lys at the sides comprising three petals, and are attributed to Edward I. From the tenth, and commonest, class, which commenced around 1301, there are two petals. This class spans the two reigns, with classes 11-15 belonging to Edward II (1307-1327).

40. Silver groat of Henry IV, 1421-61; Calais mint, *c*.1422-27.
The groat was reintroduced, successfully, by Edward III in 1351. Together with gold coins (from 1344) valued at 6s 8d (80d: the noble), 3s 4d and 1s 8d, it fitted a system of reckoning based on the mark of 13s 4d (160d, or two-thirds of a pound). From 1363 to 1403 and again between 1422 and 1440 there was an important mint at Calais (VILLA CALISIE on this coin) - held by the English and the site of the wool staple - which recoined foreign money used to buy English wool. The development of control or privy-marks in later medieval coinage is well illustrated by Henry VI's coins. Successive issues were marked with symbols, here small annulets (rings) in the legends and the main designs.

41. Venice, silver soldino of doge Michele Steno, 1400-13.
Caerleon, Monmouthshire

42. Brabant, silver double patard of Charles the Bold, 1467-77. *Bodelwyddan, Flint*

Royal exchanges at London and Canterbury were well placed to exclude foreign coins from English circulation, but two classes are found regularly throughout England and Wales. Venetian *soldini* arrived with the annual trading fleet and found ready acceptance as halfpennies ('galyhalpens'), since these were always in short supply. Their distinctive design includes, on the reverse, the winged lion of St Mark. Since their intrinsic value was closer to a farthing, the government took great pains in its attempts to suppress them.

By contrast, double patards from Flanders and Brabant (present-day Belgium) were made legal tender in 1469 as part of a political and commercial pact. They were exactly equivalent to English groats and circulated as such in England and Wales until the 1530s.

TUDORS AND STUARTS, 1485 - 1714

From the time of Henry VII (1485-1509), English coinage started to take a recognisably modern appearance, with realistic portraits, heraldic reverses, new lettering and, in due course, marks of value and dates. New denominations reflect both the availability of larger amounts of precious metal and increased use of the pound as a unit of account. Experiments to develop mechanised minting processes took place, notably under Elizabeth I (1558-1603) and Charles I (1625-49), but satisfactory techniques were not finalised until the middle of the seventeenth century. The Royal Mint at the Tower of London, from 1553 the only permanent English mint, was converted to mechanical coining in 1662.

From 1544, serious debasements, driven by Henry VIII's insatiable need for money, marked a break in English monetary tradition, but fine silver coinage was restored in 1551 and the base monies were recoined soon after Elizabeth I's accession.

By the later sixteenth century, silver small change had become impossibly small both to manufacture and for convenient use, at a time when the demand for petty currency was increasing. From 1613 the manufacture of token farthings was licensed to a succession of entrepreneurs; official currency in copper was finally introduced in 1672.

Wales, showing principal places mentioned in the text

43. Silver groat of Henry VII, 1485-1509, London.

Among Henry VII's monetary innovations were the first coins of twenty shillings (the gold 'sovereign' of 1489), the first shilling, or testoon, of twelve pence (1504) and the introduction of naturalistic profile portraits.

44. Debased testoon of Henry VIII, 1509-47, Bristol 1546-7.

From 1544, successive debasements produced large incomes for the king and profits for his mintmasters, but took the silver coinage as low as 25% fine. This period saw the first large issues of testoons. Their silver-enriched surfaces soon wore at the high points, revealing baser metal beneath, and gaining for Henry the nickname 'Old Coppernose'. The Bristol mint, last active under Edward IV (1464-83), was one of several opened for the purpose. Its master, Sir William Sharington, was convicted in 1549, amongst other charges, of falsifying the mint's records. He threw himself on the king's mercy and was pardoned.

45. Silver groat of Mary, 1553-4.

The last major issues of groats took place between 1554 and 1561. These remained important circulating coins well into the following century and are often found in extremely worn condition. Groats of Philip and Mary (1554-8) bear both of their names, but only Mary's portrait. (Their larger silver shows them facing each other.)

46. Sixpence of Elizabeth I, privy-mark Ermine and dated 1572. *Prestatyn hoard, North Wales*

A major recoinage of the debased silver monies, in 1560-1, produced mainly shillings, for minting convenience. Thereafter, for over twenty years, the more useful sixpence was the largest silver coin issued. This and its fractions (3d, 1½, ¾d) bore both privy-marks and dates, as well as a rose beside the Queen's portrait, all intended to distinguish them readily from groats, half groats and pennies. Like Mary's groats, Elizabethan silver had a long lifetime in circulation (see **58**).

47. Penny of Elizabeth I, privy-mark A, 1583-5.
48. Three-farthings of Elizabeth I, privy-mark coronet and dated 1567.

Following England's rare experience of debasement under her father, Elizabeth was reluctant to sanction small change of billon (base silver) or copper, which would have made manufacture and use more convenient. One experiment of her reign was the use of 'odd' coins such as ¾d (as change for a penny in a purchase worth a farthing), but these coins - still hand-made and of varying size - were hard to distinguish, despite deliberate design differences.

49. Shilling of James I, privy-mark Fleur-de-lys, 1604-5. *Prestatyn hoard*

The personal union of England and Scotland under James I (1603-25) was expressed on coins in his titles - from October 1604 he styled himself 'King of Great Britain' - and by the addition of the arms of Scotland and Ireland. The exchange rate now stood at 12 Scots: 1 English, so coins such as this circulated conveniently in both countries, the 'XII' representing pence in England, but shillings in Scotland. The right/left-facing alternation of the royal effigy (compare **48, 50**) has continued to the present day.

Aberystwyth Castle, by H. Gastineau, *c.*1829 *(NMGW, Department of Art)*

50. Half-crown of Charles I, privy-mark Triangle-in-circle, 1641-3. *Penybryn hoard, near Wrexham*

The first silver half-crowns (2s 6d) were struck in 1551, but it did not become a common coin until the 1630s, following a political arrangement whereby Spanish silver was coined in large quantities at the Tower. The privy-mark was usually changed annually, but this was overlooked in 1642 when civil war broke out, so the triangle-in-circle is by far the most commonly encountered. The uncertainties of the time led to the hiding of numerous hoards, some of which were not recovered by their owners, so half-crowns and the shillings and sixpences of Charles, James and Elizabeth survive in large numbers. From 1639 to 1642 a mint at Aberystwyth Castle, run by the entrepreneur and mining contractor Thomas Bushell, coined small amounts of newly-mined Cardiganshire silver. Bushell and his staff served the King at several temporary wartime mints.

19

51. Newark besieged, shilling 1645.

As the tide of the Civil War turned against the royalists, several of their strongholds endured long sieges. At a few the local governor, acting on his own initiative, issued emergency money made from silver plate, for use within the garrison. This shilling still bears traces of granular decoration from the original article. Newark, a key fortress, was assaulted three times, its coins belonging to the final siege of November 1645 - 8 May 1646.

52. Copper token farthing, James I 'Lennox' type, 1614-25.
53. Copper token farthing, Charles I 'Rose' type, 1636-44.

A royal patent for manufacturing token farthings was granted in 1613 to John, Lord Harington of Exton, and subsequently passed through several hands, including the Duke of Lennox. The tokens, made 'exactly and artificially of copper, by engines and instruments', bore the king's name and titles, but were not legal tender, depending for their acceptance on a modest profit for their purchasers (21s worth of tokens for 20s money) and a general need for small change. The tokens were nominally redeemable, but successive patentees were reluctant to accept their predecessors' issues. The basic design of **52**, which was varied from time to time, appeared in the names of James and Charles. The 'Rose' design, introduced in 1636 in response to widespread counterfeiting, incorporated a small brass plug in the material of the blank.

54. City of Bristol, farthing token, 1652.
55. Caerwys, Flintshire, penny token of Thomas Wynne, 'chyrurgeon', 1669.

The 'licensed' farthing tokens were suspended by Parliament in 1644, which once again created a shortage of small change. The shortfall was satisfied between 1649 and 1672 by numerous private issues made in London for local authorities and private tradesmen. The City of Bristol, pioneer producer of square copper farthings in 1577, was again a large issuer and its products are found widely in south and east Wales. The only Welsh municipal issue was the Borough of Brecon farthing in 1670.

Tokens of individual issuers - around 130 of these in Wales alone - generally circulated locally, but are occasionally found 'out of area'. Many Welsh issuers were mercers (in the country, general dealers whose main business was selling cloth), but others include a surgeon from Caerwys, whose token displays forceps, a towel and two extracted teeth. Typical of many such tokens, it includes a triangle of initials W / T M, for Thomas Wynne and his wife Martha, and the denomination (not normally specified on farthings). When regal copper coinage was finally introduced in 1672, the tokens were banned.

56. Copper farthing of Charles II, 1675.

The official halfpence and farthings from 1672 were struck on copper blanks imported ready-made from Sweden. A figure of Britannia, said to portray Frances, Duchess of Richmond, appeared for the first time since Roman coins of the second century AD, and set the pattern for British small change until decimalisation in 1971. From 1684 to 1692 there were also issues of tin coins, which like the earlier 'rose' farthings, incorporated brass plugs to deter counterfeiting. These were dated on their edges, which also bore the words NVMMORVM FAMVLVS ('the servant of the coinage').

57. 'Milled' shilling of Charles II, 1674.

The plain coinage of the Interregnum of 1649-60, which bore legends in English and the shields of England and Ireland, was suppressed under Charles II and recoined in 1661-3. In 1662, the mechanisation of rolling, blanking and coining processes at the Tower in 1662 transformed the coinage. Henceforth, truly circular coins of uniform apppearance, all dated, also bore decorated edges to deter clipping - diagonal or vertical 'graining' for smaller types, or the message DECVS ET TVTAMEN ('an ornament and a safeguard') and the king's regnal year, reckoned from 1649, on half-crowns and crowns. Occasionally, English coins were also marked to indicate the source of their metal. Here, the Prince of Wales's feathers badge indicates Welsh silver, used in small amounts from the early 1620s onwards - in practice it was added to general melts and marked coins were made in proportion to the quantity received. Other such provenance-marks include a small elephant (gold and silver from Guinea, W. Africa: Charles II) and VIGO (loot from an Anglo-Dutch expedition to Vigo Bay, Spain, in 1702: Anne). See also no.**60**.

Edge marking machine
(Didérot and D'Alembert,
Encyclopédie, 1771)

58. Clipped sixpence of Elizabeth I.
   Maen Cowyn hoard, near Builth Wells, Powys
59. Sixpence of William III, Bristol 1697.

After 1662, the older 'hammered' coinage continued to form the bulk of the circulating currency until the 1690s, by which time it was mostly in poor state. The Great Recoinage of 1696-7 converted this into the modern 'milled' money, but a decision to exchange all old coins for new at face value, provided that they had not been clipped within the 'inner circle' of their designs, unleashed a final epidemic of clipping. The loss this entailed and other expenses were made good by a tax on windows, which was not finally abolished until 1851. Five temporary mints - at Bristol, Chester, Exeter, Norwich and York - were set up to assist the recoinage in areas remote from London, and their products identified by the addition of the mint's initial to their dies beneath the king's bust. Almost three-quarters of the recoined money was made at the Tower Mint, and these coins bear no mint letter.

Some mottoes on common English coins

POSVI DEVM ADIVTOREM MEVM
I have taken God as my helper (Edward III - Elizabeth I)

VERITAS TEMPORIS FILIA
Truth, the daughter of time (Mary I)

EXVRGAT DEVS DISSIPENTVR INIMICI
Let God arise, let (his) enemies be scattered (James I; Charles I (Civil War))

QVAE DEVS CONIVNXIT NEMO SEPARET
What God hath joined together, let no one put asunder
(James I: refers to Union of the Kingdoms)

CHRISTO AVSPICE REGNO
I reign by Christ's favour (Charles I)

IVSTITIA THRONVM FIRMAT
Justice strengthens the throne (Charles I)

THE EIGHTEENTH CENTURY

The eighteenth century was a period of plentiful coinage in gold, which in effect became the sole standard of value. Production of silver coinage was relatively small, since it was more valuable as bullion and minting at the existing standards had become uneconomic. An increasing need for small change was to lead in the 1780s and 1790s to further private token issues when the state failed to provide this.

60. Sixpence of George I, 1723 'SSC'.
61. Shilling of George III, 1787.

Eighteenth-century silver issues were a mere trickle compared with gold, augmented occasionally by special consignments, such as the bullion deposited compulsorily at the Mint by the notorious South Sea Company in 1723, or the loot from British privateering coined with dies marked 'LIMA' in 1745-6. The only significant silver issue of George III's reign (1760-1820) before 1816 was £55,459 of shillings and sixpences in 1787.

The consistency of design from Charles II's time may be noted (**57**), but these issues include the Hanoverian arms and the British royal titles at their most extensive and (on **61**) abbreviated: GEORGIUS˙III˙DEI˙GRATIA˙ / M(agnae)˙ B(ritanniae)˙ F(ranciae)˙ ET˙ H(iberniae)˙ REX˙ F(idei)˙ D(efensor)˙ B(runsvi-censis)˙ ET˙. L(uneburgensis)˙ D(ux)˙ S(acri)˙ R(omani)˙ I(mperii)˙ A(rchi)˙ T(hesaurarius)˙ ET˙ E(lector)˙ : 'George III by the Grace of God

King of Great Britain France and Ireland, Defender of the Faith, Duke of Brunswick and Lüneburg, Arch-Treasurer of the Holy Roman Empire'. The French title, dating from the Middle Ages, was by now nominal and was dropped in 1801. The Holy Roman Empire of the German Nation was abolished in 1806. The title 'Defender of the Faith' was conferred on Henry VIII in 1521 by Pope Leo X.

62. Gold 2,000-reis (half moidore) of John V of Portugal, 1716.
63. English brass weight for a Portuguese 'Joe', after 1750.

During the eighteenth century a continuing trade surplus with Portugal, Britain's oldest trading partner, was funded by Brazilian gold, and unrecoined Portuguese gold coinage was permitted to circulate in Britain. There were two series: the moeda d'oro ('moidore') worth 27 shillings, its half (13s 6d: **62**, struck at Bahia, in Brazil) and quarter (6s 9d); and the peça, or 'Joe' (from the names and portraits of John V (1706-50) and Joseph I (1750-77)) of 36s, this series running from 72s (£3 12s) down to 4s 6d. The coins themselves are found occasionally in England and Wales, but the weights made for checking them survive today in large numbers.

Manually-operated coining press, typical of the 17th-18th centuries
(Didérot and D'Alembert, *Encyclopédie*, 1771)

64. Halfpenny of George II, 1753.
65. Halfpenny of George III, 1774.
66. 'Evasion' halfpenny, 1790s.
Although there were considerable issues of copper coins under George II, between 1729 and 1754, and George III, from 1770 to 1775, production remained irregular and quantities insufficient. Older copper circulated until worn flat and supplies were supplemented by extensive counterfeiting - even by the use of blank copper discs. One notable expedient, in the mid 1790s, involved the issuing of 'coins' with fictitious legends (and thus not strict copies), of which numerous varieties include the names of William Shakespeare, Alfred the Great and 'Louis the Sixteenth'.

67. Gold Guinea of George III, 1794.

The Guinea is relatively uncommon today, but important in that it gave its name to a much-used alternative unit of reckoning. It was introduced in 1663 as a coin of twenty shillings, but briefly reached 30s in the currency uncertainties of the early 1690s. It settled in the long term at 21 shillings (£1.05), the 'guinea', a name that survives, for instance, in horseracing circles. The most familiar of all guineas, perhaps, is the 'spade' type (named from the shape of the shield on the reverse), which was introduced in 1787, and formed the prototype for countless brass counters made in the nineteenth century (see **119**).

INDUSTRY AND WAR, 1787 - 1816

By 1787, demand for coins had outstripped supply and in the case of copper the public took the law into its own hands. Led by Thomas Williams, since 1778 controller of the rich copper mines on Parys Mountain, near Amlwch (Anglesey), many industrialists and traders had tokens made to pay their workmen, or for local circulation. Ten years later Matthew Boulton received a government contract to supply copper coin of the realm from his new steam-powered 'Soho' mint in Birmingham.

In 1797, the Bank of England suspended payments in gold, because of the French war. Because of high bullion prices, silver remained uneconomic to coin. To overcome this shortage, the Bank first countermarked Spanish silver dollars for British circulation and subsequently produced its own token silver coinages. Further private issues of tokens, both silver and copper, followed in 1811.

Thomas Williams, the 'Copper King', by Sir Thomas Lawrence, 1789 (*NMGW, Department of Art*)

68. Copper penny token, Parys Mines Company, 1787.
69. Copper halfpenny token, John Wilkinson, 1787.

The first and most prolific of the late-eighteenth
century token issues, 'Anglesey' pennies of 1787, 1788
and 1791 came to have wide circulation beyond the
company's immediate mines and smelting works. In all
250 tons of pennies and 50 tons of halfpennies were
struck for the company, mainly in Birmingham. The issues
of the Shropshire ironmaster John Wilkinson, which bear his
own portrait, also commenced in 1787.

Because of their popularity, both tokens were widely
copied, both for circulation and as varieties for
collectors. Genuine Anglesey tokens were
redeemable for coin of the realm in London,
Liverpool or Anglesey, at the company's offices: this is
stated on the edges, as a continuation of the reverse
legend 'we promise to pay ...'. Wilkinson's tokens were
redeemable at his works at Bradley, Snedshill and Willey, and at
Bersham (near Wrexham).

70. Halfpenny token, John Morgan, Carmarthen, [1792].
71. The 'Glamorgan Halfpenny', 1795.

These are two Welsh examples of the private issues of the 1790s which
followed in the wake of the Parys Mines tokens.
John Morgan issued five tons of his halfpennies, the designs of which give a
vivid picture of a contemporary
ironworks, depicting the
tapping of a furnace and,
on the reverse, the work-
ing of refined iron using
a tilt hammer. In
addition to his
Carmarthen works,
Morgan had forges at
Kidwelly, Whitland,

Cyfarthfa Ironworks,
Merthyr Tydfil, c.1820
vignette by Penry Williams
from a £1 banknote.

Blackpool (near Narberth) and Cwmdwyfran, north of Carmarthen. Often found in worn condition, these tokens clearly played a useful rôle in local circulation.

No.**71**, with its Welsh legends and 'medieval' date, often causes confusion. It was a joint issue of several Glamorgan ironmasters. An initial delivery of 100,000 in July 1795 was followed by an order for William Taitt (Dowlais), Richard Crawshay (Cyfarthfa) and Samuel Homfray (Pen-y-darren). Iestyn ap Gwrgan(t), the last native lord of Glamorgan, was dispossessed by the Normans in the early 1090s. The reverse, a version of the regal halfpenny design, reads 'the King and the Law' and bears the true date of issue. The words 'GLAMORGAN HALFPENNY' appear on its edge.

72-76. Penny, 1797; Halfpenny, 1799; Farthing 1806; Penny 1807; Halfpenny for Ireland, 1805.

In 1797, the Government finally decided upon a new issue of coppers, and placed an order with Matthew Boulton, a manufacturer who with his partner James Watt had developed new coining-presses, powered by steam, at his 'Soho' Works in Birmingham. The new penny (**72**) and twopenny pieces, soon nicknamed 'cartwheels', contained their full value of copper metal, 1 and 2 ounces respectively, i.e. 16d to the pound Avoirdupois. They were legal tender up to one shilling. The halfpennies (**73**) and farthings which supplemented them in 1799 were struck to a slightly lower standard (18d to the lb), because of a rise in the price of copper; these were legal tender up to six-pence.

Boulton's coppers were struck from dies prepared by C.H. Küchler, with the blanks held in a collar which imparted perfect circularity. The raised rims, with the lettering inset, were intended to minimise the effects of wear. The word SOHO appears in very small letters beneath Britannia's shield. The issues of 1797-9 totalled £282,138 of which the cumbersome 2d pieces accounted for £6,018 only (722,180 pieces).

Boulton's final issue, 1805-7, consisted of pennies (**75**), halfpennies and farthings (**74**), dated 1806 and 1807, to a total value of £403,193. The price of copper had in the meantime risen again, so these pieces were struck at 24d to the pound. Corresponding denominations were struck for Ireland (e.g. the halfpenny, **76**), lighter still to match the established exchange of 13d Irish for one English shilling. Irish 'harp' pennies and halfpennies circulated extensively in England and Wales - and are frequently found. Results of a survey by the Mint in 1857 suggested that almost one in every eight of the circulating copper coins was Irish.

77. Shilling token of John Voss, 1811.
78. Penny token, Cambrian Pottery, Swansea, 1813.

Continuing shortage of all coin led to another rash of token issuing in 1811, this time including silver. Private individuals such as John Voss, a Swansea banker and draper (who had in 1796 issued halfpenny tokens of the same design) put into circulation token shillings which contained around nine to ten pence worth of silver. They thus paved the way for acceptance of a token silver coin of the realm a few years later, though the immediate government reaction was the Local Token Act, which banned them from 20 December 1814.

Copper tokens of 1811-13 were predominantly pennies and often of a more utilitarian design than previously. Welsh issuers include the Flint leadworks, a woollen mill at Glanclywedog (near Llanidloes), two Carmarthen tradesmen, the Cambrian Pottery and Samuel Homfray's Tredegar Iron Co., an enigmatic token identified only by the company's T I C monogram. Several English copper companies with smelting works in South Wales also issued tokens. A local firm, the Nantrhydyvilais Air Furnace Co. at Landore, near Swansea, concerned (ahead of its time, and unsuccessfully) with the recovery of metals from waste products, issued a penny token in 1813. The copper tokens were banned from 1 January 1818.

79. Bank of England, one shilling and sixpence token, 1811.

In previous attempts to alleviate shortages, the Bank of England had countermarked (in 1797) and subsequently overstruck Spanish dollars (in 1804), to circulate at 4s 9d and 5s respectively. Between 1811 and 1816, partly as a response to the local silver tokens, the Royal Mint, newly moved to Tower Hill and equipped with steam-powered presses, coined silver tokens of 3s and 1s 6d for the Bank. The values were chosen to emphasise their token status and avoid conflict with existing silver coinage. Production of almost £3.5 million was nearly twice the amount of official silver coinage thought to be in circulation in 1811. The Bank tokens, unsurprisingly, were widely counterfeited.

The New Tower Hill Mint
(*Royal Mint*)

80. One shilling, truck ticket, Pen-y-darren 1800.

Another monetary expedient of the time should be included, though surviving specimens are individually far from common. Many industrial concerns were located in remote areas, without the ready access to goods and services that is taken for granted today. A natural development was for companies to run shops to serve the needs of their workforce and families. 'Truck' was the practice of providing goods on credit against wages (which were paid every four weeks), using paper 'cheques', and eight south Welsh ironworks went further and issued copper 'tickets' such as this, from 1800. This useful (but illegal) system was, however, open to abuse by the ironmasters in the form of compulsion to take the tickets, or high prices in the shops. The Truck Act of 1831 banned their use, but the practice was not finally ended until 1887.

ANNO PRIMO & SECUNDO

GULIELMI IV. REGIS.

✳✳

C A P. XXXVII.

An Act to prohibit the Payment, in certain Trades, of Wages in Goods, or otherwise than in the current Coin of the Realm. [15th *October* 1831.]

WHEREAS it is necessary to prohibit the Payment, in certain Trades, of Wages in Goods, or otherwise than in the current Coin of the Realm; be it therefore enacted by the King's most Excellent Majesty, by and with the Advice and Consent of the Lords Spiritual and Temporal, and Commons, in this present Parliament assembled, and by the Authority of the same, That in all Contracts hereafter to be made for the hiring of any Artificer in any of the Trades herein-after enumerated, or for the Performance by any Artificer of any Labour in any of the said Trades, the Wages of such Artificer shall be made payable in the current Coin of this Realm only, and not otherwise; and that if in any such Contract the Whole or any Part of such Wages shall be made payable in any Manner other than in the current Coin aforesaid, such Contract shall be and is hereby declared illegal, null, and void.

Contracts for the hiring of Artificers must be made in the current Coin of the Realm;

II. And be it further enacted, That if in any Contract hereafter to be made between any Artificer in any of the Trades herein-after enumerated, and his Employer, any Provision shall be made directly or indirectly respecting the Place where, or the Manner in which, or the Person or Persons with whom, the Whole or any Part of the Wages due or to become due to any such Artificer shall be laid out or expended, such Contract shall be and is hereby declared illegal, null, and void.

and must not contain any Stipulations as to the Manner in which the Wages shall be expended.

4 G

III. And

MODERN COINAGE

The recoinage of 1816-17 set the pattern for British coins of the nineteenth and twentieth centuries. Gold was the sole standard of value, expressed in a new coin of twenty shillings, the sovereign. The silver, though now token, nevertheless remained at sterling fineness (925/1000) until the disruptions of two great wars led to its reduction to 500/1000 in 1920 and its replacement by cupro-nickel from 1947. Britain finally came off the gold standard in 1931, so all modern circulating-coinage is token, though the colours of the alloys of British decimal currency continue to hint at the precious metals formerly in use. Since 1860 all bronze and since 1893 all circulating 'silver' coins have included clear statements of their face values.

Decimalisation of the currency, on 15 February 1971, formed a decisive break with the past, establishing a pound worth 100 (new) pence. Continuing developments reflect inflation (one pound coins from 1983; the demise of the half penny in 1984; smaller sized 'silver' from 1990) and political and technological progress, as moves towards a single European currency and alternative methods of cash transfer gain momentum.

Boulton steam-powered
coining press (*Royal Mint*)

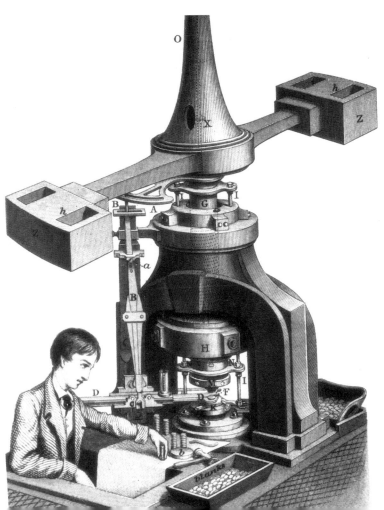

81. Two shillings (Florin) of Victoria, 1849.

The florin was introduced in 1849 as a first step towards decimalisation, as its reverse makes clear. This first issue is perhaps better remembered for its nickname 'Godless', acquired because the words DEI GRATIA ('by the grace of God') and FID: DEF: ('Defender of the Faith' - see **61**) were omitted. The Florin was a success. Its cupro-nickel descendants struck under George VI and Elizabeth II continued to circulate with the new decimal 10 pence pieces until these were replaced by a lighter version from 1992. However, an experiment with double florins (4s) from 1887-90 foundered because these were too easily confused with silver crowns (5s).

82. Copper penny of George IV, 1826.
83. Unofficial model penny, about 1848.

Official minting of copper coins resumed in 1821 and small change continued to be made from the metal until 1860. As well as pennies, halfpennies and farthings, smaller fractions are sometimes encountered: half- and quarter-farthings (for use in Ceylon) and third-farthings (for Malta). Half-farthings were also made current in the United Kingdom in June 1842. Unofficial 'model' pennies, this one by the medallist Moore of Birmingham, were made in the 1840s in an attempt to influence coinage development - the idea being to make a much lighter coin which included a silver centre to bring its intrinsic value up to one penny.

84. Bronze penny of Victoria, 1863.
85. Bronze farthing of Edward VII, 1906.

The copper coinage was superseded by lighter bronze issues from 1860, and was demonetised on 31 December 1869. The early bronze issues had a new royal portrait, with a hairstyle which gave rise to the expression 'bun penny'. The new bronze coinage remained current until 1971. The three main values (1d, ½d and ¼d) all bore the same basic reverse design until 1937. Occasionally production was again contracted out: bronze coins of Victoria of 1874-6 and 1881-2 signed H below their dates were made by Ralph Heaton & Sons in Birmingham. The same company (by then the Mint, Birmingham Ltd) made pennies of George V in 1912 and 1918-19. Pennies of 1918-19 signed KN were made by the King's Norton Metal Company.

Between 1897 and 1918, farthings were issued with a dulled and darkened finish to prevent confusion between new coins and the similarly-sized gold half-sovereigns, which until 1895 had different portraits from the farthings.

86. Silver Maundy Money of Victoria, 1899.

'Maundy Money' comprises specially-minted sets of silver coins of 4d, 3d, 2d and 1d, which are distributed annually by the King or Queen to the 'elderly poor', men and women, the numbers of each corresponding to the monarch's age. The ceremony, which takes place on Maundy Thursday, may be traced back to Saxon times and has its origins in the commemoration of Christ's washing of the feet of his disciples [John, ch.13] and until the time of James II (1685-88) included the actual washing of the recipients' feet by the monarch. The Royal Maundy is held at a different cathedral each year and worthy recipients are chosen from names submitted within the local diocese. Each receives two purses, one containing the special coins (their value in pence matching the monarch's age) and the other money in lieu of gifts of food and clothing which were formerly given. In 1982, the Maundy took place at St David's, Pembrokeshire. Maundy Money, unchanged in design by decimalisation, continues to be struck in sterling silver.

87. Silver threepence of George V, 1927.
88. Nickel-brass threepence of George VI, 1937.

The twelve-sided base metal threepence was an innovation of the proposed coinage of Edward VIII, which was frustrated by his abdication in December 1936. Introduced for George VI in 1937, it superseded the silver version in 1942. The plant, appropriately, is a thrift, though this design was replaced by a portcullis for Elizabeth II.

89 - 90. Bronze halfpenny, 1967 and farthing, 1953, of Elizabeth II.

These two reverse designs were also intended for Edward VIII, but introduced under George VI and continued for Elizabeth II. The farthing, overtaken by inflation, was demonetised in 1960 (the writer's earliest numismatic memory) and the halfpenny in August 1969, in preparation for the new decimal currency. The last pre-decimal currency issues were dated 1967.

91. Gold sovereign of Edward VII, 1903M (Melbourne).
Llanafan, Cardiganshire, hoard

The sovereign became a coin of international status, and this was underlined by the discovery of gold in Australia. A branch mint was opened at Sydney in 1855 and from 1871 it was allowed to strike coins of the same design as the Royal Mint, but with a small mint-mark (S) indicating their origin. It was followed by new branches at Melbourne (M, in 1872: here, above the date) and Perth (P, 1899). These and other smaller imperial branch mints produced nearly 500 million sovereigns and half-sovereigns in the years to 1932. From 1891 a British policy of continuous withdrawal and recoinage of under-weight gold served to cement the sovereign's reputation.

For much of Victoria's reign, British gold coins bore a heraldic reverse design, but from 1871 the 'St George' reverse by Benedetto Pistrucci, first used in 1817, was reintroduced and from 1887 all sovereigns were of this type (the halves changed in 1893).

Everyday use of gold came to an abrupt halt in 1914. With the outbreak of the Great War on 5 August, the public was urged to give up its gold. The sovereign's place was taken by Treasury notes, but some hoarding was inevitable. A brief return to the gold standard in 1925 ended in 1931. Minting was revived in 1957 to satisfy a continuing demand for sovereigns as bullion coins, notably in the Middle East, the source of large-scale counterfeiting. Special forces operating behind Iraqi lines in the Gulf War of 1991 were issued with sovereigns as part of their survival kits.

92 - 94. Shillings of George VI: 500/1000 silver, 1937 ('English') and cupro-nickel, 1948 ('Scots'); sixpence of Elizabeth II, 1967.

Many modern British coins include regional symbols in their designs. Shillings ('bobs') with English and Scottish reverses were produced concurrently from 1937 to 1966 (though both were 'United Kingdom' issues). Wales has been less well represented, though the leek appeared from 1953 as part of the designs of sixpences, florins and crowns (see **94-95**). Since 1971, the Prince of Wales's feathers badge on 2p coins, and the regular rotation of regional designs for the £1 coins have rectified this. 'Welsh' £1 coins bear the edge inscription PLEIDIOL WYF I'M GWLAD - 'Faithful am I to my country'.

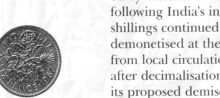

The change to cupro-nickel took place in the coinage of 1947, for silver was needed to help repay massive wartime loans from the USA. The title IND: IMP: (Emperor/Empress of India) was adopt-ed by Victoria in 1876; it disappeared from the coinage in 1949 following India's independence in 1948. The robust cupro-nickel shillings continued to circulate after 1971 as 5 pence pieces until demonetised at the end of 1990, the year in which **93** was taken from local circulation. The popular 'tanner', too, remained current after decimalisation, as 2½ new pence, following controversy over its proposed demise. In the event, demand for it dropped rapidly and with inflation eroding its usefulness, as automatic machines ceased to require it, it ceased to be legal tender on 30 June 1980.

95. Crown (five shillings), 1953, Coronation of H.M. Queen Elizabeth II.

The large size of the silver (latterly cupro-nickel) crown lends itself to commemorative issues, which do not generally find their way into circulation. In 1977 demand for the 'Silver Jubilee' crown (by then 25 new pence) was only satisfied when over 37 million had been struck. Since 1990 commemorative 'crowns' have been produced as £5 coins.

96. Half-crown, 1966.

For many years the largest circulating coin, the half-crown was a major casualty of decimalisation. Its value of 12½ new pence was thought to be inconvenient in the new system, so it was gradually withdrawn during 1969. This spurred an accelerated programme of conversion of cigarette vending machines and launderettes, where it was widely used. The half-crown was demonetised at the end of the year.

Modern coining presses at Llantrisant
(*Royal Mint*)

The Royal Mint, Llantrisant, near Cardiff; opened in December 1968 to cope with the demands of the changeover to decimal currency. The Tower Hill mint finally closed in 1975 (*Royal Mint*)

97. Fifty New Pence, 1973, Accession to the European Economic Community.

In 1973 Britain acceded to the Treaty of Rome, and the European Economic Community expanded from six to nine members. The 50 new pence coin produced for that event is the only true British currency commemorative coin of recent years, though another, for the 50th anniversary of the D-Day landings in Normandy circulated briefly in 1994. The word 'new' was dropped from the coinage in 1982. Nickel-brass £2 coins were introduced in 1986, again to commemorate special events, rather than for circulation, though a currency version is due in 1997.

SCOTLAND, IRELAND AND THE ISLANDS

The kingdom of Scotland produced its own coinage from the twelfth century until formal union with England in 1707. After Hiberno-Norse issues of the tenth and eleventh centuries, the currency of Ireland was controlled by the English until the new Irish Free State issued its own coinage in 1928. Close economic links, however, led Eire to decimalise its coinage in 1971, at the same time as Great Britain.

Coins of the offshore islands follow in general British types, but French influences can be seen in the denominations of early examples. The illegal 'Puffins' and 'Half Puffins' issued in 1929 by M.C. Harman, owner of Lundy Island, are occasionally encountered.

98. Scotland, silver 'Long Cross' penny of Alexander III, 1249-86. *Llanfaes, Anglesey*

Early Scots coinage shadowed the English, with similar, but distinct designs. The Short Cross, Long Cross and Sterling coinages all have Scots equivalents, but with profile effigies of the kings, and stars in the angles of the reverse crosses. This coin was struck by the moneyer Ion Cokin at Perth. The later Scots sterlings do not identify their mints explicitly. The two countries' coins mingled freely. Subsequent Scots debasements severed this link, but made for a more varied coinage than the English. See also no.**49**.

99. Scotland, copper bawbee (6d) of Charles II, 1678.

Scotland adopted billon (base silver) and copper coinage earlier than England, and copper issues of James VI, Charles I and Charles II are all common. The bawbee was the exact equivalent of the English halfpenny, and occasional finds in Wales show that it circulated as such. Its motto NEMO ME IMPVNE LACESSET ('no one shall hurt me with impunity') has been revived for the edges of modern £1 coins with 'Scots' designs (1984, 1989 and 1994).

100. Ireland, halfpenny of Edward I, Waterford. *Caernarfon*

The English produced coinage for Ireland at mints at Dublin, Cork, Waterford and elsewhere. These include pennies and halfpennies in the name of John (1199-1216; cf. no.**35**). Long Cross and Sterling types parallel the English, but with the characteristic addition of a triangular frame on the obverse.

101. Shilling for Ireland, James I, 1604-7.

This coinage, restoring fine silver after debased Irish issues of the Tudors, was made at the Tower Mint. These 'harpes', only threequarters the weights of their English equivalents, were also legal tender in England and Wales, but at 9d and 4½d. They are found regularly, notably in hoards of the Civil War period. The harp which gave them their contemporary nickname is a prominent feature of nearly all post-medieval Irish coinage (see also **76**).

102. 'Gunmoney' half-crown of James II, September 1689.

Expelled from England in 1688, James II tried to regain the throne through an invasion of Ireland the following year. He lacked funds, so issued an official token currency, made from brass, etc, from old cannon and other scrap metal. It was intended to exchange this for silver in due course after the war, so the coins each bore the month and year of issue, for phased redemption. At this time, the year began on 25 March (Lady Day), so December 1689 preceded January 1689, while coins of March 1689 and March 1690 were produced in the same month. In April 1690, sizes were reduced because of shortage of metal. The 'brass money' ('gunmoney' is a later description) was demonetised by William III in 1691, and even the Jacobite defenders of Limerick that year restruck them as halfpennies and farthings.

103. Jersey, copper one-thirteenth shilling, 1841.
104. Guernsey, copper 4 Doubles, 1856.

These coins, the equivalents of the British penny and half-penny respectively, owe their denominations to French traditions, in Guernsey's case the *double tournois* of the seventeenth century. In Jersey until 1877 the coinage was based on the pound of 26 *livres*, each of 20 *sous*. The Jersey penny (of 2 *sous*) was therefore one-thirteenth of a shilling. Jersey's coins always bear the monarch's portrait; Guernsey's, apart from commemoratives, only since 1985.

The twentieth-century coinages of Jersey, Guernsey and, since decimalisation, those of the Isle of Man and Gibraltar have for the most part been struck to the same standards as those of the United Kingdom, and their coins (and those of Eire) are accordingly found occasionally in change on the mainland.

SOME FOREIGN AND COLONIAL COINS

The coins that follow are among the commonest and most typical of overseas issues, but the scope of foreign coinages is so large that these can provide only a small sample. Many 'western' style coinages are often, up to a point, self-explanatory, but in other parts of the world different scripts, traditions of coinage and approaches to coin designs and manufacture make for many unfamiliar specimens. Some came to Britain in trade, others as bullion or, in the case of copper, as scrap metal. Still others came to these shores as curiosities, or souvenirs of tourism, or of civilian or military service overseas.

105. France, 'bell-metal' 2 sols, Louis XVI, 1792.
This coin belongs to the period of 'constitutional monarchy' between the revolution of 1789 and the abolition of the French monarchy in September 1792. Coinage was made from the metal of bells from suppressed religious houses. Unlike England, France still had a number of provincial mints: W beside the date identifies Lille. On the reverse is the republican emblem, fasces surmounted by a cap of liberty. The legends, in French, are 'Nation, Law and King' and 'year 4 of liberty' - dated from the capture of the Bastille in Paris on 14 July 1789.

106. France, bronze 10-centimes of Napoleon III, 1854 A (Paris).
107. France, 10-centimes 1856 K (Bordeaux), with counterstamped advertisement.
Bronze 10-centime coins of the Second Empire are commonly found in England and Wales. They were close in size to the new British bronze coinage (no.**84**) and were known as 'French pennies', circulating in large numbers in the 1870s and 1880s, as did 5-centimes (as halfpence) and similarly-sized coins from Italy, Luxembourg and Spain. They were finally prohibited in 1887 and officially bought in at post offices at a rate of 13 'pennies' to the shilling. Meanwhile, they provided advertisers with a useful loophole in the Coinage Offences Act of 1861, since while the defacing of British and Colonial coins was punishable by penal servitude or imprisonment, it was not illegal to deface foreign bronze coins. Common examples of this form of advertisement include Lloyd's Weekly News, Pears Soap and the Empire Theatre, which opened in London's Leicester Square on 17 April 1884.

108. Spain, countermarked 8 maravedis of Philip III, 1606.

Countermarking has frequently been used as an official method of revaluation or re-validation of a coin or its adaptation to a different monetary system (for instance the Bank of England countermarks of 1797). The plentiful sixteenth and early seventeenth century Spanish copper coinage underwent repeated revaluations as a result of inflation under Philip IV (1621-65). This coin of Philip III (1598-1621), struck at Segovia in 1606, was revalued at 12 maravedis at Madrid in 1641. Other specimens may bear multiple countermarks, which can be very hard to read.

109. Mexico, silver 8 reales (dollar) of Charles IV of Spain, 1793.

Spanish-American dollars ('pieces of eight') were produced in immense quantities in Peru, Bolivia and Mexico from the sixteenth century onwards and numerous modern national currencies are derived from them. In the Far East, the dollar became the preferred trading currency. Chinese merchants and bankers, used to treating coins as bullion ingots, applied their own marks (known as 'chops') to coins to show that they had tested them for weight and fineness. A number may be seen on this specimen. These Carolus dollars are also the types which were countermarked and restruck by the Bank of England in 1797 and 1804 respectively.

110. Silver 'Maria Theresia' taler, dated 1780.

The English name 'dollar' was in use by 1600, derived from the German term 'Taler' for the large silver coins struck by numerous states from the sixteenth century on. The best known of these is the 'Maria Theresia' taler. The Austrian mint at Günzburg was opened in 1764 to make talers for the use of Augsburg bankers in financing trade with the East. By 1780 talers of the empress Maria Theresia were already highly valued in the Yemen and Arabia and demand continued after her death that year. By 1783 existing dies had worn out, so new ones of identical design

were authorised. Many millions have since been struck at Vienna and (at various times down to the 1960s) at Milan, Venice, Brussels, Paris, London (20 million between 1936 and 1961), even Bombay (in 1940-1). The vast majority of 'Maria Theresia talers' are therefore modern restrikes, and identifying their sources and dates depends on minute details, since their designs have remained unchanged since 1780.

111. Ionian Islands, copper one-fifth obol (lepton), 1834.
112. British West Africa, cupro-nickel halfpenny of Edward VIII, 1936.

Colonial coinages might adopt local denominations and systems (e.g., in India), adapt existing coins, such as the countermarking and cutting up of Spanish silver in the West Indies, or employ the monetary system of the colonial power, as happened in British West Africa. Two British colonial curiosities are illustrated here, the appearance of Britannia and the lion of St Mark on a 'Greek' coin and a currency issue of Edward VIII.

The Ionian Islands, which include Corfu, Cephalonia and Zante, belonged to Venice until its empire ceased in 1797. They were then administered successively by France, Russia/Turkey and France again before becoming a British protectorate in 1815 until 1863, when they passed to the Kingdom of Greece. The British Ionian islands used a decimal system beased on the Spanish dollar of one hundred obols, with small change produced in London. The first issues were too large for local tastes and were replaced in 1834.

Edward VIII's (Jan.-Dec. 1936) British coinage was never issued, because of the lengthy process of design and approval, though by the time of his abdication trial specimens had been made. For certain colonial coinages, on which a central hole precluded the use of the King's effigy, all that was needed were small changes of inscription or design, and considerable quantities of coins for East and West Africa, Fiji and New Guinea were struck and issued during 1936.

113. Morocco, brass 3 fals, 1286 H (AD 1869-70).

This coin, with its apparent Star of David, 'medieval' date and unclear arabic inscription, regularly causes confusion. The date is in fact of the Mohammedan era, reckoned in lunar years (11 days shorter than calendar years), which began in AD 622 with the *Hijra*, Mohammad's flight from Mecca to Medina. The inscription gives the mint name, here Fez. These coins were made by casting in strips, and the weakness of some details and mark of breaking at the edge are characteristic.

114. China, brass cash, Qianlong era, AD 1736-96.
Everyday coinage in China before the twentieth century took the form of cast copper-alloy cash, threaded on strips, nominally by the thousand. Those of the emperor Qianlong ('Ch'ien Lung' in the former transliteration) are among the most commonly encountered. On the obverse (left) his name appears top and bottom, together with characters meaning 'current money'. On the reverse a manchu inscription identifies the mint, here the Board of Works, Peking, one of two in the city (the other being the Board of Revenue).

PARANUMISMATICA

This term was created in the 1970s as a blanket description for coin-like objects which do not fit into conventional numismatic categories such as coins and medals. These range from medieval reckoning-counters, nineteenth-century whist counters and advertising tickets (including items such as **105**), to modern gaming machine or telephone tokens. Again, only a small sample of the commoner types is featured here.

Reckoning with counters and using Arabic numerals, 1543
(*Douce Prints C19, f221, no776, by permission of the Ashmolean Museum, Oxford*)

115-118. Jettons (reckoning counters): English; French; Flanders; Nürnberg, Hans Krauwinckel.

Jettons are coin-like discs made from copper alloys, often of latten - a form of brass with a bright yellow colour resembling gold - and rarely of precious metals. They were principally made during the later Middle Ages and early modern period, in Northern and Central Europe: in England (early fourteenth century, **115**), France and the Low Countries (fourteenth-fifteenth centuries) and the German city of Nürnberg (later fifteenth century on).

Designs are often simplified versions of contemporary gold coins and instead of the names of rulers, etc., the legends may be religious (e.g. AVE MARIA GRATIA PLENA, as **116**), explanatory (**117**: 'Jetton of good latten') or a nonsensical combination of letters. The 'orb-in-trefoil' design is characteristic of Nürnberg jettons and from the mid-sixteenth century onwards these are mainly of a stock type (e.g.**118**), giving the maker's name, the most frequently-encountered being Hans Krauwinckel the younger (1586-1635). Reverses bear religious or other mottoes: on **118**, 'today red, tomorrow dead' (i.e., here today, gone tomorrow). Jettons were sold in sets for use in computation, rather in the manner of an abacus, on tables or cloths marked for the purpose. It is sometimes suggested that they may also have served unofficially as small change, but there is no conclusive evidence for this. Their use in computation died out early in the seventeenth century with the widespread adoption of arabic numerals, but production of jettons for other purposes, e.g. as card-counters, has continued.

119-120. Spade Guinea and Half-guinea Counters

Brass counters bearing designs copying the British regal gold coinage of the late eighteenth and nineteenth centuries are among the commonest numismatic objects shown for identification. They were made by a variety of manufacturers, mostly in Birmingham, and were intended for use in card-games. Two main 'families' are described here.

The 'Spade' guinea of George III, so-called from the shape of the shield on the tail side, was issued from 1787 to 1799. The first counters copying this guinea were made from about 1788; to avoid charges of forgery, some were given wavy edges and bore manufacturer's initials, e.g. W A & Co. (Wilmore, Alston & Co.). Later, when the guinea had long been obsolete, large numbers of imitations, often quite crude, were made. These occur with legends such as IN MEMORY OF THE GOOD OLD DAYS (e.g **120**) or with the name, address and business of the Birmingham manufacturer in abbreviated form, e.g. G.Y.I.ET.F.G.REX.S.UF.ST. D.S.T.M.S.ET.E. (George York Iliffe and Frederick Gardner' [REX from the original legend] 'Suffolk Street, Die Sinkers, Tool Makers, etc.', **119**) and there is generally an arbitrary eighteenth - century date, occasionally anachronistic, e.g. '1701' . Sometimes the maker's name is given in full, for instance C.H.A.R.L.E.S. P.E.V.E.R.E.L.L. E. M.A.K.E.R. B.I.R.M. Other issues served to advertise firms such as the London grocer J. Sainsbury, whose business originated in Drury Lane. Trade directories show that such counters were made in the period 1860 - 1910. 'Mute' types, i.e. with no maker's name or advertisement, continued to be made until the 1940s.

121-122. Counters imitating Victorian Sovereigns.

These have the head, name and modified title of Queen Victoria on one side. On the other, many have the figure of a man on horseback, crowned and with sword erect, riding over a two or three-headed dragon, with the legend TO HANOVER and the date 1837 . The design symbolises the departure of Ernest Augustus, Duke of Cumberland, the unpopular eldest uncle of Queen Victoria, who became King of Hanover in 1837 on the accession of Queen Victoria to the throne of Great Britain. Hanover's Salic law prevented the succession passing to a woman whilst a male relative of the preceding ruler (William IV) was still alive. Hanover was absorbed by Prussia in 1866. These counters were issued from about 1837 onwards.

These counters were sovereign-size and so long as the current sovereigns bore a shield on their reverse, there was little danger of confusion. However, after the 'George and Dragon' design (first used under George III and IV) was reintroduced in 1871, the 'To Hanover' counters were frequently passed off as sovereigns and their manufacture was finally prohibited in 1883, though prosecutions for uttering them continued until 1890. A related series of sovereign-size counters bears designs explicitly related to card-play: a group of cards (**122**), or a player at table, with the legend KEEP YOUR TEMPER.

123. Prince of Wales model half sovereign.

These have a similar head side; the reverse bears the Feathers badge of the Prince of Wales and his motto ICH DIEN (I serve), all within a collar, crowned, and the legend THE PRINCE OF WALES MODEL HALF SOVRN. The future Edward VII was born in 1841, and was made Prince of Wales. The counters appeared in 1842 and continued down to about 1875. They do not resemble any official issue of half-sovereigns.

124. Advertising token: John Jones, Swansea 1840.

Between 1820 and 1870, partly in response to continuing inadequate supply of regal copper, numerous tradesmen and others issued 'advertisement tickets' which served conveniently as unofficial farthings in local circulation. John Jones was a linen and wollen draper at 28 Castle Street, Swansea. Another South Wales issuer (1839) was 'Baron Spolasco' (real name J. Smith), a flamboyant and popular quack-doctor in Swansea (1838-45) and elsewhere.

125. Threepenny check, George Inn, Tredegar, Mon., *c*.1860.

Pub checks ('tavern tokens') are metal tokens issued by retailers of beers, wines and spirits. They were used in several ways, for instance as 'wet rent', whereby friendly and benefit societies agreed to buy a certain amount of drink in exchange for the use of a room, or as combined admission and refreshment tickets for entertainments or games. Participants received checks which essentially ensured the compulsory purchase of beer, the largest source of the publicans' profits. The practice went back at least to the early nineteenth century, but most brass checks of this type belong to the second half of the nineteenth and early twentieth centuries, and most were made in Birmingham. Typically, the checks identify the establishment, the landlord and their value; sometimes there is a pictorial design. A few are dated, otherwise Trade Directories are helpful for approximate dating.

126. Penmaenmawr, Gwynedd, Co-operative & Industrial Society, £1 dividend check.
127. Newport, Mon., Co-op Society, 2lb bread check.

The co-operative movement of the nineteenth and twentieth centuries has given rise to numerous checks. These may relate to dividends, which depended on the amounts spent by individual members (as recorded on **126**), mutuality trading (a form of credit), and prepayment for specific items such as coal, bread, or milk, which helped make deliveries more efficient and guarded against cash losses.

128. Re-engraved Half-crown of William III.

Secondary uses of coins include their incorporation into jewellery, and their use as mementoes, usually involving defacement. The eighteenth and nineteenth centuries saw widespread engraving of worn or obsolete coins as tokens of affection, or as items of remembrance - recording for instance a death, or enforced separation (such as transportation). The engraving might be of a high standard, or very crude. Other defacements might be overtly political, such as a chisel-cut on the neck of Louis XVI of France, or the initials of sectarian organisations (UDA, UVF, IRA) stamped on coins circulating in Belfast, Northern Ireland, in the early 1970s.

129. Brass weight for a 'Laurel' of James I.
130. Brass guinea weight by William Abdy, about 1773.
Where modern token coins require consistent weights in order to function in machines, coins of previous centuries depended for their value on their precious metal content. The weights used to check them, usually made of brass, survive in large numbers. They are characteristically thick, may be square or round and often bear a version of the design of the coin to which they relate, as **129**: the 'Laurel' of James I was a gold coin of twenty shillings introduced in 1619, which took its name from the laurel wreath of the king's portrait. A series of Acts of Parliament between 1773 and 1776 re-introduced a 'least current weight' for guineas of 128 grains (5 pennyweights 8 grains) - the full legal weight was 129½ gr. Withdrawal of light coin was phased, so other weights were set for earlier coins to remain current for a short while: 5dwt 6gr (guineas of 1760-71) and 5dwt 3gr (pre-1760). These measures gave rise to extensive series of coin weights for guineas and their halves and quarters. Abdy was a London goldsmith. See also no.63.

131. Brass half-sovereign weight, Royal Mint, 1843.
Weights for the new sovereigns and halves, with minimum legal weights of 5dwt 2½gr and 2 dwt 13⅛gr respectively were first made in 1821. In 1842 William Gladstone, the Master, insisted that a minute discrepancy in the Mint's standard weights (3/100 of a grain for the sovereign), first noticed in 1825, be put right. A new series of weights was therefore issued in 1843.

NOT WHAT THEY SEEM

Counterfeiting is almost as old as coinage, and fakes have formed a steady feature of currencies throughout history, not only in the 'epidemics' of unofficial production of small change when supplies were inadequate (e.g., **17**, **53**, **68**ff.), but also through the fraudulent production of inferior precious-metal issues. With the growth of collecting came forgeries to deceive collectors; concoctions and altered dates (most famously numerous '1933' pennies); and replicas, some produced for the best of educational reasons, others purely for commercial purposes.

132. Counterfeit noble of Henry VI.
White Castle, Monmouthshire
This coin has been struck in a lead alloy by dies which copy, with reasonable accuracy, a gold noble of Henry's 'annulet' issue of 1422-27 (see **40**). It would then have been gilded to pass for 6s 8d (80d), but this seems not to have happened here. It appears that this 'coin' spoiled in the making and was therefore discarded. Was White Castle the home of a fifteenth-century den of coiners?

White Castle from the air (*Cadw: Welsh Historic Monuments. Crown Copyright*)

133. Counterfeit half crown of Charles II, dated 1677. *Caerleon, Monmouthshire*

This coin, made of a copper alloy with a silvery coating, would have made a quick profit for its maker before the surface wore off. It was recognised and nailed through to take it out of circulation. Other sources of profit to the coiner included the use of base silver alloys whitened by the addition of arsenic, and issuing light weight coins, especially before mechanisation made individual coins more uniform.

134. Counterfeit sixpence of George III, dated 1818.

This is a very good copy, but made of brass. Public unfamiliarity with a new coinage is always a good opportunity for the illicit coiner, and there are plenty of false examples of George III's last coinage of 1816-20. Despite the relegation of modern coinage to a token rôle in small transactions, counterfeiting remains worthwhile if profits outweigh costs. The Fifty Pence and One Pound decimal coins have been widely faked.

135. Electrotype replica of a silver dekadrachm of Syracuse; late nineteenth century.

Electrotyping produces a precise replica by the deposition of copper onto a mould taken from a genuine coin, forming a 'shell', which is then filled with a low melting lead alloy. 'Electros' may be one-sided, and therefore obvious, but they are often joined to form very convincing 'coins', which are then patinated or given the appropriate metallic finish. Often, however, there is a clear line on the edge which shows the join, and on this example the initials 'RR' which identify Robert Ready, who made many electrotypes of coins in the British Museum between 1859 and 1897, for educational purposes.

136. Cast replica of an Antioch tetradrachm of Nero.

This 'coin' was one of a series made in 1964-5 for Nicholas laboratories of Slough, promoting an antacid called Polycrol. Packs headed 'If you had been a physician in ...' were given to doctors. They contained a replica coin (here, of the Roman emperor Nero, AD 54-68), historical information and details of the firm's new product. These replicas are obvious casts, with uneven surfaces, weak detail and a raised line on the edge where the moulds met (the original coins were struck). Most modern replicas bear some indication that they are such, but this may be removed. One series sold in museums, etc., has the letters 'WRL' stamped into the surfaces: these are made by Westair Reproductions Ltd, of Birmingham. Others marked 'CADW' are sold at certain historical sites by Cadw: Welsh Historic Monuments.

COMMEMORATIVE MEDALS

Medals commemorating persons or events grew in popularity from the Renaissance onwards, reaching their heyday in Britain in the nineteenth and early twentieth centuries. Most are coin-like, produced by the same processes of striking or casting, and while they tend to be larger and more carefully made, smaller medals are often confused with coins. Those most commonly encountered are souvenirs of royal events: coronations, jubilees, visits. Others may be purely of local significance. A small selection of medals with Welsh connections is illustrated here.

137. Victoria, Golden Jubilee, 1887: Bronze cross, St Asaph.
138. Coronation of King Edward VII, 1902: 'white metal' medal, Wrexham.
These are two North Walian examples of the numerous local medals given to schoolchildren on the occasions of important national royal events. The St Asaph item is an obvious imitation of the Victoria Cross, Britain's highest award for gallantry, (though the red ribbon is probably a later private addition).

The Wrexham medal retains its red-white-blue ribbon: often these and their mounts are missing, but a small piercing at the top of a medal shows that these would originally have been present. 'White metal' is an alloy of tin.

(reduced)

139. The Alexandra Dock Medal, Cardiff, 1907.

Perhaps the most commonly shown commemorative medal, this was produced by (or for) the Cardiff goldsmiths Spiridion and Son of 29 Duke Street. It commemorates the Royal visit and opening of the Queen Alexandra Dock on 13 July 1907. Examples of the medal in copper were distributed to Cardiff schoolchildren by the Lord Mayor, Sir W. S. Crossman, apparently in September of that year. Rarer examples exist in silver, some at least of which were sold to collectors by Spiridion at fifteen shillings each - one of these was purchased by the collector R. D. Roberts of Bethesda, Caerns., on 27 September 1907 and is now in the National collection.

140. Investiture of Edward, Prince of Wales, Caernarfon, 1911.

There have been formal investitures of two princes of Wales in the twentieth century, both at Caernarfon Castle, where Edward I first 'presented' a prince to the Welsh people. That of Edward (VIII) took place on 13 July 1911. This official medal for the occasion was designed by Sir William Goscombe John, and produced in gold and silver. Charles, Prince of Wales, was invested on 1 July 1969, an occasion which gave rise to more than fifteen official and unofficial medals.

141. Barry Arts and Crafts Exhibition, 1910: silver prize medal.

The 1910 Barry (Glamorgan) Arts and Crafts Exhibition took place from 22 October to 2 November in aid of the Y.M.C.A. and the Seaman's Institute (British & Foreign Sailors Society). Essentially a local event, it nonetheless attracted 2,500 loan exhibits and 1,000 competition exhibits in 14 sections, including entries from Essex and Motherwell (Scotland). At least 145 of these medals, by Vaughton of Birmingham, appear to have been awarded (four in gold, 66 silver and 75 bronze). The four horticulture classes produced three silver medals for 'J. Woodward' and 'Mrs Woodward', who also won a medal for breadmaking.

142. National Museum of Wales: Opening of the Courtyard Galleries, 1993.

The National Museum of Wales was founded in 1907, and first opened to the public in 1922, with a formal opening by King George V in 1927. An ambitious design by the London architects Smith and Brewer was never realized in full, because of financial constraints. Instead, piecemeal building over the years was united and completed by the 'Courtyard' development initiated in 1988, which was opened by H.M. Queen Elizabeth II on 15 October 1993. This event was marked by a medal designed by the Welsh artist and engraver Robert Evans and produced at Llantrisant by the Royal Mint. A gold example was presented to the Queen; 40 silver (**142**) and 500 bronze were given to members of committees and staff.

The obverse depicts the façade of the National Museum at Cathays Park, Cardiff. On the reverse (*enlarged*), the new galleries are represented schematically, 'cut' into the field, and overlain by symbols representing the five subject departments in the building: Archaeology and Numismatics (an early medieval brooch of Welsh type); Art; Botany (the Welsh poppy); Geology (a fossil trilobite from Mid-Wales); and Zoology (the Red Kite). These are united by 'Celtic' snakes - symbols of eternity and of protective beneficence.

Robert Evans at work (*Royal Mint*)

51

TWO WORLD WARS

The scale of the World War of 1914-18 went well beyond that of any previous conflict, and it gave rise to the issue of millions of campaign, gallantry and commemorative medals. Unlike those of any other country, Britain's campaign medals had since the early nineteenth century been impressed with the names, ranks and units of their recipients. The specimens described here illustrate British campaign and service medals, the official commemoration of those who died and the use of medals as propaganda.

Service in the Second World War (1939-45) was marked by a series of campaign 'Stars', a general War Medal and the Defence Medal. However, these were mostly issued unnamed.

143-145. 1914-15 Star; British War Medal; Allied Victory Medal.

(reduced)

There are two British 'stars' for service in the Great War. The 1914 Star, sometimes incorrectly called the 'Mons Star', was awarded for service in France or Belgium between 5 August and 22 November 1914. In 1919, the King sanctioned the award of a bar '5TH AUG.-22ND.NOV.1914' for all who had been under fire in France/Belgium during this period; it was worn sewn to the ribbon. About 366,000 1914 Stars were issued, with 145,000 bars. The 1914-15 Star (**143**) was awarded to all those who had seen service in a theatre of war between 5 August 1914 and 31 December 1915, apart from those eligible for the 1914 Star. About 2,078,000 were issued. Each of these stars is named on the reverse. The ribbon, shared by both, is of watered silk: red, white and blue in equal stripes, the colours merging into one another. Recipients of either always received in addition the British War and Victory Medals, giving the 'standard' Great War trio known colloquially as 'Pip, Squeak and Wilfred'.

The British War Medal (**144**: reverse shown) was instituted by King George V in 1919 to mark the end of the Great War and record approved active service between 5 August 1914 and 11 November 1918 (Armistice Day), later extended to cover operations in Russia during 1919 and 1920. About 6½ million were issued in silver; a further 110,000 in bronze were given to Chinese, Maltese and other subsidiary 'native' units. The ribbon is an orange central band flanked by white, black and blue stripes. The giving of bars for certain battles and theatres of operations was discussed and 68 for naval recipients and 79 for the Army were suggested. The naval bars were approved in 1920 and a few made for wear with miniature medals, but the idea as a whole was dropped in 1923 because of the expense involved. Most, but not all, recipients of the War Medal also received the Victory Medal.

The Allied Victory Medal (**145**) was authorised in 1919 to commemorate the victory of the Allies over the Central Powers and to obviate the exchange of Allied commemorative war medals; it covered, in the main, service up to November 1918. Each country issued its own medal, but each bore a classical figure of a winged victory and a ribbon with the colours of the rainbow was also common to all. About 5¾ million of the British Medal were issued. All recipients also received the War Medal. A specimen of the Victory Medal with a bronze oakleaf attached to its ribbon signifies that its recipient was 'mentioned in Despatches' for some meritorious service in action.

The Welsh Division at Mametz Wood, 1916, by Christopher Williams
(*NMGW, Department of Art*)

146. The Great War Memorial Plaque.

In October 1916 the Secretary of State for War, David Lloyd George, set up a Government Committee to consider what form of memorial should be distributed to the next of kin of servicemen who had died. It was decided that the cost would be borne by the State and by August 1917 a competition was announced for the design of a memorial plaque, to be cast in bronze. Over 800 entries were received. The winning design, by Edward Carter Preston, comprises the figure of Britannia, helmeted and robed, holding a wreath in her left hand and supporting a trident with her right. In front of her a male lion faces to the viewer's right. Behind and above her, two dolphins symbolise the importance of British naval power. At the bottom of the plaque, a lion pounces on an eagle, which symbolises the enemy powers.

(reduced)

The plaques, which are 4¾ inches (12 cm) in diameter, were mostly cast at 'The Memorial Plaque Factory', which was set up in a disused laundry in Acton, West London. Each was named individually, by embossing the names of the dead on thin steel strips which were held in place on a master model by an electro-magnet as each mould was prepared.

The plaques commemorated those who died in all theatres of war, or from related causes, between 4 August 1914 and 30 April 1920; the total number produced may have been as great as 1,150,000. Each was accompanied by a memorial scroll and a short covering letter bearing the facsimile signature of King George V.

147. The 'Lusitania' medal, 1915: British replica, cast iron.

The German artist Karl Goetz produced a running commentary on the Great War in the form of a series of propagandist and satirical medals. One such, seeking to link the sinking of the liner Lusitania off Ireland on 7 May 1915 to the shipping of armaments from America, drew a rapid response, which speaks for itself. The common British version may be distinguished from the German by the spelling 'May' for 'Mai'.

Please do not destroy this

When you have read it carefully through kindly pass it on to a friend.

A
German Naval Victory

"With joyful pride we contemplate this latest deed of our navy. . . ."—
Kölnische Volkszeitung, 10th May, 1915.

This medal has been struck in Germany with the object of keeping alive in German hearts the recollection of the glorious achievement of the German Navy in deliberately destroying an unarmed passenger ship, together with 1,198 non-combatants, men, women and children.

On the obverse, under the legend "No contraband" *(Keine Bannware)*, there is a representation of the *Lusitania* sinking. The designer has put in guns and aeroplanes, which (as was certified by United States Government officials after inspection) the *Lusitania* did *not* carry; but has conveniently omitted to put in the women and children, which the world knows she *did* carry.

On the reverse, under the legend "Business above all" *(Geschäft über alles)*, the figure of Death sits at the booking office of the Cunard Line and gives out tickets to passengers, who refuse to attend to the warning against submarines given by a German. This picture seeks apparently to propound the theory that if a murderer warns his victim of his intention, the guilt of the crime will rest with the victim, not with the murderer.

Replicas of the medal are issued by the Lusitania Souvenir Medal Committee, 32, Duke Street, Manchester Square W. 1.

All profits accruing to this Committee will be handed to St. Dunstan's Blinded Soldiers and Sailors Hostel.

148-151. The Second World War: 1939-1945 Star; Africa Star; War Medal; Defence Medal.

Eight British campaign stars and two service medals were awarded for the war of 1939-45, though no one person could wear more than five of the stars. The 1939-1945 Star was basically awarded for six months operational service during the period and was normally supplemented by stars specific to certain theatres of war: Atlantic; Africa; Pacific; Burma; Italy; France and Germany; Air Crew Europe. Bars sewn to the ribbons might denote either that the recipient was entitled to two stars which were not authorised to be issued together (e.g. Atlantic/Air Crew Europe/France and Germany ; Pacific/Burma) or refer to a specific service (examples are BATTLE OF BRITAIN on the 1939-1945 Star and 8TH ARMY on the Africa Star). King George VI took an active interest in the the stars, notably in designing the colours of the ribbons, chosen to symbolise aspects of the award in question. The stars are made of bronze.

The War Medal (**150**: reverse shown) was awarded to full-time personnel of the armed forces, for 28 days' service at home or abroad. The obverse bears the crowned head of King George VI. The ribbon is of red, white and blue stripes, and a bronze oakleaf on it signifies 'Mentioned in Despatches' or receipt of the King's Commendation for Bravery. The Defence Medal (**151**: reverse shown) bears the uncrowned head of the King. The ribbon is flame-coloured with green edges, with thin black stripes (symbolising the black-out) on the green ones. The medal was awarded to the numerous men and women who served in Civil Defence, Home Guard, Mine and Bomb Disposal units, Police, the Fire Service, etc. The War and Defence Medals are made of cupro-nickel, except for Canadian issues in .800 fine silver.

(reduced)

ACKNOWLEDGEMENTS

I am grateful to the Ashmolean Museum, Oxford, to Cadw: Welsh Historic Monuments and to the Royal Mint, for permission to reproduce copyright material; to Tony Daly for the maps; to Tony Hadland and Jim Wild for photography; and to Richard Brewer, Graham Dyer, Nick Mayhew and Lucy Olive for advice and encouragement.

FURTHER READING

The literature of numismatics is vast, but the following works are suggested as being useful to develop aspects of the highly condensed summaries above. Some are out of print, though they should be accessible through libraries.

Burnett, Andrew
Interpreting the Past: Coins; 1991

Cribb, Joe (editor)
Money: from Cowrie Shells to Credit Cards; 1986

Porteous, John
Coins in History; 1969

Williams, Jonathan (editor)
Money; a History; 1997

Rutter, N.K.
Greek Coinage; 1983

Nash, Daphne
Coinage in the Celtic World; 1987

Burnett, Andrew
Coinage in the Roman World; 1987

Casey, P.J.
Roman Coinage in Britain; 1980

Besly, Edward
Roman Coins relating to Britain; 1987

Brooke, G.C.
English Coins; 1932 (reprinted 1966)

Oman, Sir Charles
The Coinage of England; 1931

Seaby, P.
The Story of British Coinage; 1985

Dyer, G.P.
The Royal Mint: an Illustrated History; 1986

Dyer, G.P.
Royal Sovereign 1489 - 1989; 1989

Mays, James O'D.
The Splendid Shilling: a social history of an engaging coin; 1982

Besly, Edward
Coins and Medals of the English Civil War; 1990

Boon, George C.
Welsh Tokens of the Seventeenth Century; 1973

Boon, George C.
Welsh Industrial Tokens and Medals; 1973
[18th - 19th centuries]

Mathias, Peter
English Trade Tokens; 1962

Mays, James O'D
Tokens of Those Trying Times; 1991
[19th cent. silver tokens]

Bateson, D.
Scottish Coins; 1987

Edge, Brian
The First Dictionary of Paranumismatica; 1991

Biggs, Norman
English Weights: an Illustrated Survey;1992

Cox, Noel and Alan
The Tokens, Checks, Metallic Tickets, Passes and Tallies of Wales 1800-1993; 1994

Fearon, Daniel
Victorian Souvenir Medals; 1986

Joslin, E.C. and others
British Battles & Medals; 1988